My Monster Mungo

A Story About Imposter Syndrome

Written by AJ Lauer, EdD

Illustrated by Chelsey Hill

My Monster Mungo: A Story About Imposter Syndrome
Published by Bin Chicken Press
Superior, CO

ISBN: Hardback: 979-8-9923942-0-7
Paperback: 979-8-9923942-1-4
Ebook: 979-8-9923942-2-1
BUSINESS & ECONOMICS / Workplace Culture

Illustrations by Chelsey Hill, chelseyhill.com; Cover and interior design by Victoria Wolf, wolfdesignandmarketing.com; Publishing management by KLR Literary Management. Copyrights owned by AJ Lauer.

The examples, anecdotes, and characters in this book are drawn from my work and life experience with real people and events. Names and some identifying features and details have been changed, and in some instances people or situations are composites.

This book is not intended as a substitute for the medical advice of trained clinicians or therapists. I do not make guarantees about the results of the information included in the book because your success or failure will be the result of your own efforts, situation, and other circumstances.

QUANTITY PURCHASES: Schools, companies, professional groups, clubs, and other organizations may qualify for special terms when ordering quantities of this title. For information, email hello@thrivingibis.com.

For my little monsters.
— AJ

"What makes you think you'll lose the promotion from this?" Alice asked.

"The CEO is clearly going to know I fooled them into giving me this job. I'll never make Director with mistakes like that."

Alice nodded knowingly. "That sounds like your Imposter Monster talking."

Katy's jaw dropped. "My what?!"

"Your Imposter Monster. You know, that voice that makes you think you've tricked people into believing you're better than you are or that your success was solely based on luck. And sooner or later, someone will figure it out, and you'll lose everything."

Katy frowned and looked at her menu. "I'm not the only one who thinks that way?"

"Nope! I feel it all the time," Alice said. "It's called Imposter Syndrome, but I prefer to think of the voice as a Monster rather than an illness. I've actually named my monster - Moo. It's got these weird horns that look a bit like a Highland cow, but when I feel like an imposter, it feels like it's breathing fire down my neck."

"That sounds awful!" Katy shuddered.

"It's really not all that bad," Alice shrugged. "When it shows up, I feel like I can talk to it. You know, like we're in it together."

"Heyy! Hi everyone! We were discussing the terrible feeling of not being good enough, making a big mistake, fearing losing everything, and thinking your world will collapse."

"Ohh. Imposter Syndrome. Yeah, I definitely need a taco for this discussion," Thom stated as he sat next to Alice. "Pass me that menu!"

"That sounds rough," said Hugo. "I don't think I've ever experienced that. Scoot in!"

"Ugh, I feel that way all the time," agreed Ana. "Let me tell you!"

"You know I'm the first person in my family to become a doctor. I worked SO hard to get here.

But being young and a woman, people often call me a nurse. If they ask a question I can't answer or if I need more information, I feel ashamed because, as the doctor, I feel like I should know everything.

Plus, when I make mistakes, I feel like I'm letting down my whole family. It sucks."

"Oh dear," Jane said. "You know your family is proud of you, even if you make a mistake once in a while. And besides, you can't be everything to everyone — right Rey?"

Rey looked up from their phone. "Uh, right. Yeah. Sorry. I just remembered something I have to do tonight."

"I feel that, though, Ana. It's like I have to do everything on my own. I HATE asking for help," lamented Thom.

"Like, last year, when I presented my Q3 numbers to my investors. The numbers were good, but I needed their help because I couldn't get this one wholesaler to return my calls. I thought they would pull my funding because I couldn't reach the guy! I mean... who am I to be running an entire company if I need help with a tiny task like getting ahold of a vendor?"

"What happened?" Katy asked.

"They didn't seem to care," Thom said. "In the meeting, they barely acknowledged my request, but they must have done something because the next day I had a response from the vendor. I thought I'd die of shame."

But Thom, you're SO good at what you do! They would never pull funding," Katy said reassuringly.

"I mean... I would hope so, but I'm a middle-class Black man, and my funders are all uber-rich white guys. ...I know there's part of themselves that expects me to fail. Some days, it's hard not to let that get in my head."

"Hey Thom - if you had to picture that feeling as a monster, what would it look like?" Alice asked.

"Ohh... Something blue and globby. With antennae that pick up on the smallest hint of discomfort. I'd call it Glub."

"Thom, if I had a friend like you in the room when I'm doing presentations, I'd be so much more comfortable," Katy said miserably.

Jane patted Katy's hand. "You know, I used to be a perfectionist like you, Katy. But at my age, I've realized that dwelling on every mistake I've made along the way wouldn't leave any room for happiness."

"You all make life sound so awful," Hugo said. "I just try to keep things easy. Stay in my zone of genius, you know? Then I don't have to feel bad about stuff."

Rey gave Hugo a dubious look. "But what about last year when you got stuck on a coding issue for like... four months? You were so ashamed you started wearing a ball cap pulled low over your face to try to hide yourself!"

"Of course, you wouldn't understand wanting some space, Rey. You're available to everyone ALL the time. Have you even put your phone down since we've been here?" Hugo replied.

"Hey man... you don't know what it's like. Everyone keeps saying I'm this leader in the community. It's a lot of pressure.

They want me to attend events, speak at conferences, write newspaper articles... Oh and then I have to take care of my normal job, the kids, and volunteering at church.

I feel like if I fail at any of those things, I'll let everyone down and lose their respect. And then what?"

"And then," Ana stated, "we'd invite you out for tacos and figure out your next big thing!"

"Leave it to the Doc to come up with the perfect solution," Alice noted.

"Hey Thom, you need help with those tacos?" Hugo asked.

"No way! I already told you I don't like to get help with anything. Get your paws away from my food!"

The conversation turned to lighter topics as the friends finished their meals, but Katy couldn't get Alice's comment about Imposter Monsters out of her head.

The next day, Katy started to learn about Imposter Syndrome. She discovered even the most amazing individuals can feel like frauds. Like their achievements were fake and someone would "find them out" for being a phony. That made her feel a LOT better about the whole thing.

She also learned that the first researchers called it the imposter *phenomenon*—not syndrome—and said that environments were influential in creating the phenomenon in college-aged women.[1]

Despite what she'd thought based on the word "syndrome," imposterism wasn't a diagnosable illness—it was a coping mechanism to feel more comfortable within certain environments.

...despite outstanding academic and professional accomplishments, women who experience the imposter phenomenon persist in believing that they are really not bright and have fooled anyone who thinks otherwise.

Dr. Pauline Rose Clance

Dr. Suzanne Imes

Katy tried Alice's suggestion of thinking of her imposter feelings as a little monster. She closed her eyes and remembered that awful feeling she had during the presentation.

Her Monster, she realized, was blue and furry, with a sharp tooth that was just too long to fit inside his mouth. His name... was Mungo.

"Hello, Mungo," Katy said cautiously. "It's nice to meet you. Can I ask what brought you here?"

Mungo let out a growly sigh.

"I've been here since you were a kid. Remember that time when you got a bunch of questions wrong on your math test, and you were so upset?

I'm here to make sure you don't make mistakes like that again. The kind that can screw everything up."

Katy blinked in surprise. "Oh! Thanks? I guess..? But Mungo, why do you try to make me feel bad all the time?"

"I'm here to protect you, not make you feel good, kid. There's nothing worse than the shame of failure. So I figure if I keep you from doing things or make you aware that you haven't done a good job in the first place, we won't have to deal with the consequences."

"Speaking of... that presentation you've got on Monday...

How about we play video games all weekend instead of finishing the slides so you can blame any mistakes on not having time to prep? Whaddya think?"

"Mungo, that won't help me get a promotion. I've been working so hard for this! Wouldn't it be better to do a good job rather than failing on purpose?"

"I don't know, dude. This is how I've always done things. Are you asking me to change or something? That really gets my fur up..."

Katy laughed. "I don't know! Maybe we won't need to change much. How about this? We'll spend today learning how to deal with Imposter Syndrome, and then we can talk about some video games." Mungo reluctantly agreed, so he and Katy spent the rest of the day learning as much as they could about imposter feelings.

Katy and Mungo learned from Dr. Valerie Young's five competence types that all "imposters" hold themselves to impossibly high standards. But they don't all do it in the same way.

Suddenly Katy could see how her friends experienced the imposter phenomenon in *their* own ways.

The Perfectionist: Focuses on *how well* something is done.

Feels shame if they make even the smallest error.

The Expert: Focuses on *how much* they know and *how well* they know it.

Feels shame if they don't know even the tiniest detail.

The Soloist: Focuses on *who* does something.

Feels shame if they need help accomplishing things.

The Natural Genius: Focuses on *ease and speed* of accomplishments.

Feels shame if they are not able to master a subject or skill on the first try.

The Superhuman: Focuses on *how many* tasks or roles they can juggle at once.

Feels shame if they drop any balls - even small or unimportant ones.

At the end of the day, Katy said, "Mungo, it looks like I'm the Perfectionist and Expert types of imposter. I always want to have the answers and don't like making mistakes. I feel ashamed when I do. But... I want to do hard things! I want to get my promotion and make a difference in our company.

"Do you think... maybe... rather than discouraging me from doing hard things, you could say nicer things and support me?"

"How is that protecting you? I'm supposed to protect you, not help you make mistakes!" declared Mungo.

"Well," Katy mused, "this research suggests I reevaluate my definition of 'good enough.' So maybe we could try for almost-perfect and celebrate that?"

"I don't know..." Mungo hesitated, "that sounds like a pretty big change."

"Alright, let's make a deal. Let's try it for the presentation on Monday. Tomorrow we'll spend the morning reviewing the slides, and then we can play video games all afternoon. But then, on Monday, you have to remember we've agreed that I'll do my best, but it doesn't have to be perfect."

"OK, OK." Mungo conceded. "You had me at video games."

The following Friday...

"I can't believe it's taco night again! Hey, Katy, how did this week's presentation go?" Alice asked.

"Not perfect, but I'm OK with it. My Monster, Mungo, totally had my back, and I'm meeting with my boss about a promotion next week!"

The End!

TACOS

Turn the page to
learn more!

AUTHOR'S NOTE

SEPTEMBER 10, 2024

I'm sipping hot chocolate and bopping along to whatever song is on the radio at a cafe in Boulder, Colorado, while I type this. I'm also having a conversation with my Imposter Monster, Borscht, about writing this book. After all, who am I to be writing an actual BOOK about imposter syndrome?! It doesn't matter that I have my doctorate in leadership studies, or that I am a trained executive coach, or that I've successfully helped a number of clients befriend their Imposter Monsters.

I am a total phony, and someone is going to figure it out, so I may as well just chug my hot cocoa and binge Netflix.

These are classic Imposter Phenomenon feelings, all tangled up with some of my deeper fears about life and business. Yes, friends! I have them too! Before I tell you how the rest of that conversation went, let's take a moment to talk about what the Imposter Phenomenon really is and why having a Monster can help you get through it.

PARTS WORK

The idea of talking to one's Monster stems from a therapeutic tradition called parts work.[2] In parts work, clients are encouraged to recognize the different aspects of themselves that show up to protect them from their biggest fears or traumas.

For example, if deep down we are afraid that we aren't good enough, a part of ourselves may not allow us to take credit for our accomplishments. Or, if we experienced some kind of abandonment, we may have a part that shows up to ingratiate us to others hoping they stick around.

The parts that show up for protection may fall into the category of either Managers or Firefighters. If we think of our Monsters as protectors, then...

Monsters that are Managers could use self-sufficiency (or the opposite!) to keep things running smoothly day-to-day. They foresee and prepare for difficulties to help us avoid embarrassment or prevent abandonment. That might look like making us procrastinate so we can blame a failed talk on lack of preparation rather than lack of expertise. Or our Monsters may insist on absolute perfection for that talk in order to hide a lack of confidence in our competence.

Monsters that are Firefighters may react to a real or perceived danger by distracting or numbing us, using a solution to a problem without regard to consequences, creating barriers, or completely disengaging. That might look like binging on Netflix rather than responding to an interview request by the deadline. Or it may look like overspending on a fancy outfit at the last minute in order to look like you fit in at an event.

In parts work, the purpose of interacting with our parts on a regular basis is to form a relationship with them. That's why, no matter how scary a Monster is, we're not just telling them to shut up. We're acknowledging that they serve a purpose or have served a purpose in the past. While we may not exactly become friends with our Monsters, we're recognizing the wisdom they bring, and moving forward together.

IMPOSTER SYNDROME

For many of us, imposter feelings are a symptom of deeper feelings of not being good enough or unrealistic expectations of competency. This often stems from external expectations of perfectionism from the media, our parents, and our communities. It is magnified by unfair expectations and stereotypes based on race, gender, disability, being LGBTQ+, and/or holding other identities.

It's very important to note that while the term includes the word "syndrome," Imposter Syndrome is not a diagnosable mental illness.

You are not ill.

You *are* experiencing a common psychological phenomenon. If you feel those three key indicators of Imposter Syndrome (I've fooled people into thinking I am more intelligent or talented than I am; my accomplishments are due to luck or other external factors; and I'm scared other people will figure out that I am an imposter)[3] you are in very good company! Research shows that up to 82% of individuals will experience imposter feelings at some point.[4]

The key is to try to develop a more healthy view of competence (i.e. not perfectionism or being the only one who can do something!) and not feel shame when you screw up.

Your Monster can be a great tool for this. By paying attention to when your Monster shows up and what they say, you can learn a lot about what preconceived notions are holding you back. And then you can do the hard things anyway and take mistakes as a learning experience.

THE CONVERSATION CONTINUES...

When I ask Borscht what he's protecting me from, it's all the feelings wrapped around the perception of competence we assign to publishing a book. What if the book isn't good enough? (That's my Perfectionist.) What if we're not credible enough? (Hello, Expert!) Who's going to spend money on this? (Fear of failure.) What if this is a monumental failure, and you're publicly shamed, and you lose your business, and your family leaves you, and, and, and...! (Failure and abandonment fears! AHH!)

This is how the rest of the conversation went:

AJ: Borscht, what I'm hearing is that you're trying to protect me from failure here.

Borscht: Obviously! Failure would be catastrophic!

AJ: It would be embarrassing, yes. But I think you're being a little dramatic thinking that our family would leave just because I wrote an unsuccessful book.

Borscht: I guess. They stuck with you after the Cherry Debris Incident,* after all!

AJ, chuckling: They did, though they still tease me about it. Can you trust me to put my best work out into the world, and to take care of things if it doesn't go well?

Borscht: I can. But I'm going to be right here the whole time...

AJ: I wouldn't expect any less!

Through this conversation, you can see that I have no expectation or desire for Borscht to go away. He's here, he's snarky, and he's actually pretty smart. By engaging him in conversation, I felt more confident about putting this work out into the world.

My hope is that you can develop a similar relationship with your Monster. One where you aren't allowing imposter feelings to hold you back—rather your Monster helps you develop a more realistic idea of what it means to be a competent adult and move forward with doing hard things even when you're intimidated.

With a friend (or at least a non-threatening acquaintance) by your side.

All my best,

~Dr. AJ Lauer

*In which I attempted to make baked brie cheese with cherries without a recipe, and it did NOT go well.

DISCUSSION & SELF-REFLECTION QUESTIONS

LET'S INTRODUCE YOU TO YOUR MONSTER!
Grab a piece of paper and something to write and draw with.

Then quiet your mind and think about a time you felt like an Imposter. What was the voice in your head saying to you? What did they sound like? If you envision this voice as a Monster, what do they look like?

Draw your Imposter Monster. What is their name?

The defining feelings of the Imposter Phenomenon are: I've fooled people into thinking I'm more intelligent or talented than I am; my accomplishments are because of luck or other external factors; and I'm scared other people will figure out that I'm an imposter. What is your first memory of experiencing these feelings?

Which of the 5 types of imposters (The Perfectionist, The Expert, The Soloist, The Natural Genius, The Superhuman) most resonated with you?

Research shows that people develop imposter feelings due to external as well as internal pressures. What messaging did you receive from the rest of the world that pushed you toward your ideas of what competence means?

What does your Monster say to you in moments of imposterdom?

How does the idea of showing compassion toward your Monster feel?

What happens when you respond to your Monster with compassion? (try phrases that start with "I see that...", "Thank you for...", "I understand why...")

How might you open up a conversation with other people about your Monster and theirs?

FURTHER READING

For information on Imposter Monster workshops and other news, please visit my website: **www.thrivingibis.com/imposter-monsters**

If you're interested in learning more on this subject, I've compiled a list of recommended books about Imposter Syndrome and Parts Work here: **https://bookshop.org/lists/imposter-monsters-recommended-reading**

Imposter Syndrome Institute resources, including more information about the 5 Types of Imposters: **www.impostersyndrome.com/resources**

REFERENCES

1   Clance, P.R., & Imes, S.A. (1978). The imposter phenomenon in high achieving women: Dynamics and therapeutic intervention. Psychotherapy: Theory, Research & Practice, 15(3), 241–247. DOI: https://doi.org/10.1037/h0086006

2   Schwartz, R. (2021). No Bad Parts: Healing Trauma and Restoring Wholeness with the Internal Family Systems Model. Sounds True Adult.

3   Young, V. (2011). The Secret Thoughts of Successful Women (and Men). Crown Currency.

4   Bravata, D.M., Madhusudhan, D.K., Boroff, M., Cokley, K.O. (2020). Commentary: Prevalence, Predictors, and Treatment of Imposter Syndrome: A Systematic Review. J Ment Health Clin Psychol, 4(3), 12-16. DOI: http://dx.doi.org/10.29245/2578-2959/2020/3.1207

About the Author

Dr. AJ Lauer (she/her) is on a mission to improve diversity in science and technology fields. AJ deeply understands the impact STEM fields have on all of us and believes that positive culture change in organizations can change the world. Dr. Lauer has held diverse professional roles including running a residence hall, leading an educational exhibit design project, and coaching and training C-suite staff - and has the stories to prove it! Her company Thriving Ibis Leadership Solutions provides tailored workshops, retreats, individual and group training, and more to help build leadership skills and retention in the workplace.

About the Illustrator

Chelsey Hill is an illustrator based in Omaha, Nebraska. With a background in the performing arts, Chelsey's works are often inspired by eccentric New Yorkers, off-beat Nebraskans, and legendary musicians and performers.